Matthew Hancock

Xenophobe's Guides

Published by Xenophobe's® Guides

Telephone: +44 (0)20 7733 8585
E-mail: info@xenophobes.com
Web site: www.xenophobes.com

Xenophobe's® is a Registered Trademark.

First printed 2012
Revised 2013, reprinted 2014

Editor – Catriona Tulloch Scott
Series Editor – Anne Tauté
Cover designer – Vicki Towers
Printer – CPI Antony Rowe, Wiltshire

Grateful thanks are given to Luke Tilley
for his help and suggestions.

ePub ISBN: 9781908120755
Mobi ISBN: 9781908120762
Print ISBN: 9781903096840

Contents

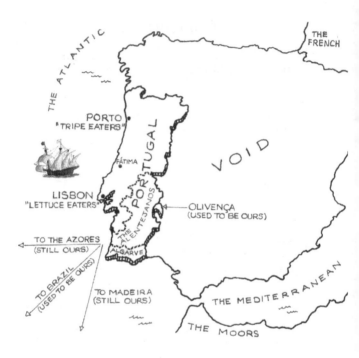

The population of Portugal is 10.5 million, compared with 47 million Spanish, 62 million British, 64 million French, 206 million Brazilians and 315 million Americans.

The bulk of Portuguese-speakers are elsewhere in the world, in the former Portuguese colonies of Angola, Brazil, Cape Verde, Goa, Guinea Bissau, Macau, Mozambique, East Timor, and the islands of São Tomé and Príncipe.

Portugal is more than twice the size of Switzerland but is one-fifth the size of Spain, and could fit into Brazil 90 times.

Nationalism & Identity

Historically the Portuguese have turned their backs on the rest of Europe and instead looked in on themselves: a tight-knit family group where formality and old-fashioned politeness remain highly prized values and where a sense of togetherness has enabled them to retain their independence. Portugal's border with Spain is one of the least changed borders in the whole of Europe: it is virtually the same as when its boundaries were defined by treaty in 1297.

Sitting on the periphery of Europe suits the Portuguese. They may be in the same school class as the southern Europeans, but they are the shy kids who sit at the back hoping not to be noticed. To be Portuguese means to be reserved: that gesticulating exuberance is left to their Mediterranean cousins. Perhaps this is because the Portuguese are never influenced by the balmy heat of the Med: their temperament is forever cooled by the Atlantic whose surf pounds their country's western and southern shores. And its eastern and northern borders are edged in by Spain, historically their rivals in love and war. Closed in on all sides, they tend to keep their heads down.

> **❝ To be Portuguese means to be reserved: that gesticulating exuberance is left to their Mediterranean cousins. ❞**

How they see themselves

The Portuguese see themselves as a giant family. A homogeneous race with no splinter groups agitating for independence or complaining about the repression of an obscure language, they will stick together on all occasions.

> **66 A homogeneous race, they will stick together on all occasions. 99**

They also see themselves as a nation of great explorers, happy to seek out pastures new when things are really tough. Portuguese communities flourish in places as diverse as Venezuela, South Africa, Luxembourg and Canada.

Fiercely loyal to each other and to their country's ways, the Portuguese consider themselves to be tolerant and open-minded. Portugal was, and still is, one of the most ethnically diverse countries in southern Europe. When the dictatorship which had governed the country for several decades ended in 1974, over half a million people from newly independent former colonies – mostly from Angola and Mozambique – knocked on Portugal's door and they were all let in. To the Portuguese, these people were not so much foreigners as overseas relatives.

When Britain handed Hong Kong back to the Chinese, it pretty much waved goodbye to the Hong Kong residents. When Portugal did the same with the neighbouring colony of Macao in 1999, it allowed any of its residents to become a Portuguese citizen.

The same has applied to Goa in India and East Timor in Indonesia: anyone who lived there before they became independent could claim Portuguese citizenship.

The peoples of its former colonies may be distant cousins with different names, but to the Portuguese, they are still part of the extended family. And they don't just receive a Christmas card once a year: they are welcome to stay at any time, for as long as they like.

How others see them

As Portugal shares the Iberian peninsula with Spain, the rest of the world generally assumes that the Portuguese are a Mediterranean race. The impression is of a land of seafaring fishermen who make good waiters and occasionally throw up good footballers; a place where people are called José, play the guitar, eat paella and grilled sardines, and once had a famous navigator called Henry.

The reality is that the Portuguese are an Atlantic race, fiercely independent from Spain. There are a lot of Josés but don't call them

> **66 The impression is of a land of seafaring fishermen who make good waiters and occasionally throw up good footballers. 99**

Hosay like the Spanish: in Portugal they are 'Jo-say'. They do listen to guitar, but to the Portuguese guitar played with *fado*, not flamenco. And their rice and seafood dish is *arroz de marisco*, not paella. So

Portugal may be like Spain, but it is certainly not a Spanish satellite.

The un-Mediterranean character of the Portuguese can come as a surprise. They are relatively quiet and easy going, an erstwhile colonial power which has absorbed a substantial number of immigrants from its former colonies with apparent ease. But though not a Mediterranean race it is still a southern European one, with the quaintness, the inefficiencies and slow-paced living that one comes to expect from a land with a sunny climate whose people are rarely hurried.

The special relationship

Portugal's special relationship with Brazil is very much like the one between the UK and the USA: a former colony that outgrew its coloniser and whose culture permeates every aspect of its founder nation. The evening schedules of a whole family can revolve around the times of the nightly Brazilian *telenovelas* (soap operas). These show the dramatic exploits of glamorous leggy women and macho hunks in exotic loca-

> **The evening schedules of a whole family can revolve around the times of the nightly Brazilian *telenovelas* (soap operas).**

tions, with the inevitable *fofoca* (scandal and intrigue), a potent mix that is so popular that to be cool you have to use a few Brazilian Portuguese expressions like *tudo bem*? (how's it going?) and *ciaozinho* (see you).

The Portuguese also find they dance better to Brazilian rhythms (all the rage in many clubs) after a few *caipirinhas*, a highly alcoholic Brazilian cocktail made with distilled sugar cane.

Until Portugal joined the EU, Brazilians could freely enter Portugal, and even today there is a healthy population of *brasileiros*, mostly the educated

> **The Portuguese are rather proud of the New World glamour Brazilians bring to Olde Worlde Portugal.**

elite who use Portugal as a stepping stone into Europe. The Portuguese are rather proud of the New World glamour Brazilians bring to Olde Worlde Portugal, though not all are happy with their cultural mores.

In addition, the Brazilians are inclined to regard the Portuguese as quaint, old-fashioned and slightly dim. And here lies the rub, or rather the Portuguese Achilles heel: a sensitivity about the attitude of people from their former colonies, especially Brazil. The *brasileiros* in Portugal are not only over-paid, over-sexed and 'over here', but are often furnished with an overweening sense of superiority. The Portuguese take pleasure in reminding their Brazilian cousins that most of their place names, their state religion and their language all came from Portugal. Anyone who claims to have shaved clean their Portuguese roots would be a bare-faced Brazilian indeed.

5

The not-so-special relationship

A Portuguese does not care to be mistaken for a Spaniard. When addressed in Spanish by a foreigner, he would rather answer in English or French. Spain is the neighbour with the big house, and the leylandii trees that block out the light. To get to the shops, Portugal has to use its drive: all land routes connecting it with the rest of Europe pass through Spain first.

> **66 The Spanish may not be the neighbours from hell, but they are neighbours the Portuguese resent. 99**

The Spanish may not be the neighbours from hell, but they are neighbours the Portuguese resent.

'Neither good winds nor good marriages come from Spain' is a well-known Portuguese saying. It is nearly 400 years since Spain relinquished its occupation of Portugal, but distrust runs deep after a history of wars and border skirmishes. Even now, many Portuguese claim the town of Olivença in Spanish Extremadura as their own, invoking a Treaty of 1815 which the Spanish seem to have conveniently forgotten.

Today, Portugal's economy hangs on to the coat tails of Spain's, and the Portuguese look with alarm when Spanish companies take over slices of their country's banking, commerce or real estate.

Yet to go to Spain is a sign of success, a step towards the Big Time. Many of Portugal's top footballers leap at the chance to play for Real Madrid;

Nobel Prize winning author Saramago left Portugal to live in Tenerife. Like the British, who are cynical about Americans but secretly hanker to be like them, the Portuguese quietly envy their larger neighbours. To counteract this, they have always attempted to keep up with the Josés – anything the Spanish state can do, the Portuguese state tries to do too. After all, when Spain's navigators colonised half the world, the Portuguese colonised the other half – the Treaty of Tordesillas in 1494 literally divided the New World in two between the Iberian nations.

A Portuguese proverb states, '*A galinha da vizinha é mais gorda que a minha*' (My neighbour's chicken is fatter than mine). So when the Spanish built the lavish palace and monastery of El Escorial in the 16th century, the Portuguese king João V decided to outdo them and commissioned an even bigger palace and convent at Mafra, north of Lisbon. It had 15,000 labourers working on it each day, and when com-

> **❝ They have always attempted to keep up with the Josés – anything the Spanish state can do, the Portuguese state tries to do too. ❞**

plete it boasted 5,200 doors and 2,500 windows. The library was stocked with so many books that when Lord Byron visited, he was asked if there were any books left in England. Unfortunately, the king's vanity successfully bankrupted the country and it has never been quite the same since.

For most of the 20th century, Portugal turned its back on its neighbours like a sulky child. Cross border traffic was not encouraged. Until it became a full member of the EU, there was merely a handful of crossings over the mountains and rivers that make up the natural border with Spain. Public buses from Portugal would stop at the border, and you had to walk across to Spain and hope that the wait for the Spanish bus was not too long: they were rarely coordinated. Before a motorway bridge opened in the 1990s, you could only go from Portugal's top tourist area, the Algarve, to Spain via a rickety car ferry at Vila Real, unless you drove to Alcoutim where the river was narrower: here you could get a man to take you across the border in his rowing boat.

> **Public buses would stop at the border, and you had to walk across to Spain.**

On television, Portugal's weather maps show the oblong of Portugal usually dotted with a sea of suns: east of Beja and north of Valença is a void where Spain should be. The meteorologist has successfully depicted what many Portuguese desire: Spain simply does not exist.

Emigrants and Immigrants

The British are aware that many Americans, Canadians and Australians with Anglo-Saxon names have some sort of British ancestry. But they would never claim Bill Clinton or Nicole Kidman as a Brit. Not so the Portuguese. If a well-known person is Portuguese by descent, he or she is to be celebrated as their own. Thus the American writer John Dos Passos (1896–1970) is widely fêted for his Madeiran ancestry. Nelly Furtado considers herself a Canadian with Portuguese forbears: to the Portuguese she is a Portuguese Canadian. And so the list goes on. Sexy American actress Daniela Ruah? She's really Portuguese. Carmen Miranda? Portuguese. Keanu Reeves? Portuguese with a bit of Hawaiian.

But the one that always stirs up passions is Christopher Columbus. He may be claimed by Spain and Italy, but any

66 **Christopher Columbus may be claimed by Spain and Italy, but any Portuguese will tell you he lived in Madeira.** 99

Portuguese will tell you he lived in Madeira, married a Madeiran girl and was only inspired to head west to the Americas after he saw things washed up on the beaches of Porto Santo, Madeira's sister island. You can take a Portuguese out of Portugal, but you can never take Portugal out of the Portuguese.

One thing all these people (or at least their ancestors) had in common was the knowledge that to get on in Portugal, you get out. From the great navigators like Ferdinand Magellan and Vasco da Gama to contemporary artist Vhils (real name, Alexandre

Farto), sports personality José Mourinho and London-based chef Nuno Mendes, to become anyone you have to go elsewhere.

The Portuguese have been 'getting out' ever since the words 'Portuguese colony' entered the public domain. Poor labourers and farmers left southern Portugal to colonise Madeira and the Azores in the 15th and 16th centuries. In the 20th century around a million Portuguese sought better lives in Australia, Canada, the US, Venezuela and South Africa. The majority emigrated to Switzerland, Germany, England and France. Paris has the largest Portuguese population of any city outside Portugal. A Portuguese joke is that Europe was the last continent the Portuguese discovered.

> **66 The Portuguese have been 'getting out' ever since the words 'Portuguese colony' entered the public domain. 99**

But the Portuguese don't move for the culture. When removed from their homeland, they are like the Brits abroad seeking out fish and chips in Marbella: the Portuguese stick together, speaking their own language, opening shops that sell dried cod and cafés that serve their national Sagres beer and pickled lupin seeds.

And unless they achieve the ultimate prize – fame and fortune – the chances are that a Portuguese's ultimate aim will be to see out his days back in the homeland. Many of Portugal's nouveaux riches who have made their fortunes abroad have returned. Yet when they do, they may feel out of place, especially as they probably want to show off their new-found wealth with a gaudy new villa. When a Portuguese complains that 'they come over here with their fancy foreign ways', it's most likely a complaint aimed not at a foreign immigrant, but at a *retornado*, a returning Portuguese.

Character

To join the big Portuguese family requires adopting a formality, an old-fashioned politeness and an understanding of the various quirks which make the Portuguese tick – though fully fathoming the Portuguese is a bit like fully understanding their language: superficially similar to many others, but actually very hard to comprehend without years of practice.

The Portuguese seem most contented when dangling a fishing rod from a cliff top, guiding the tiller of a chugging boat or soaking *bacalhau* – their

> **❝ This mild-mannered, gentle and homely race once ran an empire that stretched over half the world. ❞**

beloved, salted cod – in the kitchen sink. Yet this mild-mannered, gentle and homely race once ran an empire that stretched over half the world. To understand the Portuguese, you need to be aware of another, less obvious side to their character. Look at the paintings of the Portuguese artist Paula Rego and you will get an idea of their dual nature. From a distance, Rego's paintings of Portuguese figures are calm and hauntingly beautiful. But look close up and

66 Like their namesake, the Portuguese Man O' War, what seems placid and harmless can pack a punch. 99

you will see that her people are thick-set, grim-faced and powerful, their gestures and clothing hinting that they have a potential for something wicked, maybe even cruel. Like their namesake, the Portuguese Man O' War, what seems placid and harmless can pack a punch. Generally referred to as a 'jellyfish', it is actually a siphonophore – a creature consisting of a colony of organisms working together. It is appropriately named since the Portuguese have a similar take on life.

The sting in the tail of the Portuguese unsheathes itself when they are sitting behind the wheel of a car. Suddenly the reserved individual is replaced by a reckless, risk-taking maniac that nothing and no-one can stop from reaching his goal in as short a time as possible. The ruthlessness that rules their roads once ruled the waves and the message is: we may be the quiet boys of the school, but mess with us at your peril.

As a Portuguese, you know when to hold your ground. For example, visit a shop on the first day of the sales. Like Portuguese navigators from history, you'll try to arrive before anyone else. When the doors open, you use all powers available to gain entry. Umbrellas, walking sticks and bags are useful aids to get ahead in a throng, though elbows may be more effective. The superficially weak, small, ancient and surprisingly determined get what they want first – just like the Portuguese, in fact.

So don't expect their reserve to be a sign of civility, let alone complaisance: when put on the spot, the Portuguese usually come up trumps and get the rest of the class nodding in approval. You don't rule half the world's trade routes without having lead in your pencil.

Togetherness

The Portuguese share a bubbling sense of together-ness. You can get first-hand experience of this when-ever you visit one of the country's enormous sandy beaches. Here, should you find a secluded spot far from the crowds to spread your towel, it will only be a matter of time before other Portuguese will appear on your section of

66 The Portuguese share a bubbling sense of togetherness. 99

beach. Though they could position themselves any-where, they will invariably place their towels within a few feet of your own, reassured by the proximity of fellow Portuguese. It can be the same at a restaurant, where it is not uncommon for customers to be seated at a bench alongside fellow diners, or at a table uncomfortably close to another, even when half the restaurant is empty.

But perhaps one of the best demonstrations of togetherness is having a communal gripe about a common cause, as happened in Culatra, an elongated sand spit island off the coast of the Algarve. The residents of this vehicle-free island are all fishermen who have lived an idyllic offshore lifestyle for generations. But realizing that the mainland had mains electricity while they relied on generators, the fishermen banded together, refusing to supply fish to the hungry mainlanders until they were connected. Collective bargaining being a respected tool in Portugal, their demands were soon met. A fish-free diet for a Portuguese is akin to an Englishman being deprived of his tea.

> **❝ A fish-free diet for a Portuguese is akin to an Englishman being deprived of his tea. ❞**

Fatalism

The Portuguese word *oxalá* means 'if only' – a word that derives from the Arabic *Inshallah*, 'if god wills it', and though the Moors who ruled their land have long since departed, the Portuguese still share this que sera sera mentality with their Muslim neighbours. It is deeply embedded in their psyche and it has both negative and positive influences on their character.

The negative

Broody and moody is a temperament you would expect from a land of mist and bogs, not one with a Mediterranean climate, golden sandy beaches and plentiful wine. But while the Spanish are too busy enjoying life to worry about long-lost empires, and the British act as if they had never lost theirs, the Portuguese brood about what could have been. They experienced Golden Ages in the 16th and 18th centuries but these came to a juddering halt because of a horrendous earthquake and the vast overspend of over-ambitious monarchs. A third Golden Age has, perhaps, just ended, after funds flooding in from the EU led to Portugal being branded a PIGS*.

> 66 Broody and moody is a temperament you would expect from a land of mist and bogs, not one with golden sandy beaches and plentiful wine. 99

To the Portuguese, all this was inevitable, since fate will always take things away: they even have a word for this, *saudade*, a feeling of longing for what could have been, a nostalgia for what has gone. Even the

*A term used since the mid-1990s to refer to Portugal, Italy, Greece and Spain – noted for their troublesome economies.

15

national form of music, *fado*, takes its name from 'fate': a melancholy, soulful music that the Portuguese describe as pure emotion – and the uninitiated describe as woeful wailing. Perhaps only the Portuguese could relish the proverb, 'There is a remedy for everything; it is called death.'

The positive

Luckily, to believe in fate like a Portuguese is also to believe that anything is possible – Lisbon rose again from the earthquake, Golden Ages will come again. If things are bad, you may as well enjoy yourself while you can, even if it means borrowing money up to the hilt. Or you can do as the Portuguese have always done: disperse across the seas to see what might be found, knowing that fate will guide you back to the mothership sooner or later.

❝ Even the national form of music, *fado*, takes its name from 'fate': a melancholy, soulful music that the Portuguese describe as pure emotion. ❞

Furthermore, if anything is possible, you can be hugely inventive. It was the Portuguese who perfected the caravel in the 1400s, a sleek vessel capable of sailing close to the wind allowing it to go faster and further than any other of its time. They devised navigational devices to find their way around the oceans, opening up sea routes to boldly go where no man had gone before. They also claim to have invented an early

16

flying machine: a Jesuit priest, Bartolomeu de Gusmão, allegedly got his machine airborne in 1709, and though the Portuguese king was impressed, the invention was not pursued – only the inventor was, by the Spanish Inquisition, for his ungodly creation.

Everyman

Every Portuguese has a bit of Zé Povinho in them. Zé Povinho is an everyman figure created by satirist Rafael Bordalo Pinheiro in 1875 when – not for the first or last time – Portugal's economy was going down the drain. The country's elite gave no say to Portugal's commoners, so Bordalo Pinheiro created his Joe Bloggs cartoon figure to mock the bumblings of the ruling classes. Zé Povinho – literally 'Joe Little Person' – is poor, keen to help others, and ruthless in his criticism of the rich and powerful. The Portuguese empathise with the character to this day, displaying a courteous respect for authority but only up to a point: the little man won't be pushed about when times are tough. Hence the occupation of

> **66** Zé Povinho is poor, keen to help others, and ruthless in his criticism of the rich and powerful. **99**

Portugal by the Spanish was tolerated until they tried to squeeze too much from the Portuguese troops who in 1640 booted them out once and for all. Likewise, in 1910 the Portuguese royal family was ditched for losing touch with the common people.

The Portuguese may have a brightly coloured cockerel as a national symbol, but their attitude to fashion sums up the plain view of the average man: clothes are for keeping you warm in the winter and cool in the summer. Elderly men wear faded brown suits. Elderly women wear black. Businessmen wear grey suits, or perhaps jeans with a jacket and tie if they consider themselves artistic. Women wear various shades of brown. Things have moved on since Bordalo Pinheiro's cartoons, but you can still see plenty of country folk wearing a baggy white shirt with a brown leather waistcoat and a brimmed hat. The Zé Povinho everyman look is alive and well.

Attitudes & Values

Desenrascanço

The Boy Scouts' mantra is 'Be Prepared'. The Portuguese have a diametrically opposite philosophy: Don't plan, just improvise. They have a word for it, *desenrascanço*: literally 'disentanglement', an unplanned grapple to get yourself out of a sticky situation. So if you're stuck in the middle of a forest and don't know where you are, you won't have a compass or emergency rations. You will plan on the hoof and eat moss and follow the sun. The result may be a total failure, but you will have pitted your wits against the odds and winged it to the last.

Desenrascanço is plugging a gap in your fence with a road sign or mending a punctured football by sticking a rose thorn in the hole. The Portuguese believe this is an essential life skill. Indeed university freshers are often posed unnecessary practical problems to solve by their teachers as part of their initia-

> **❝ *Desenrascanço* is plugging a gap in your fence with a road sign or mending a punctured football by sticking a rose thorn in the hole. ❞**

tion ceremony, to see how capable they are of thinking on their feet. Likewise new soldiers joining the armed forces.

To be adept at *desenrascanço* is an inbuilt part of being Portuguese, and they are fiendishly good at it. After all, the great navigators in history could not possibly be prepared for the situations in which they found themselves when they pulled up on the shores of previously undiscovered lands. Ad hoc, haphazard, last-minute *desenrascanço* was, and is, the only way to get out of life's little tangles.

Love of animals

Dogs are part of the scenery in Portugal. In towns they are often fashion accessories – poodles and pomeranians with pink collars and leads, led by elderly ladies in fur coats; or powerful black pedigrees led by important looking men in suits. The dogs live in flats, which means their outdoor spaces consist of a balcony or small patio where they will make their presence known by loud yapping whenever anyone passes. Some dogs' exercise consists of being led downstairs to the nearest patch of pavement, where they'll water the local tree before being taken back inside.

Country dogs are altogether freer, if less pampered. These are kept outside pretty much permanently, seeing off anyone who approaches their patch. When they are not on their patch, they will potter about quite happily, trotting across roads and wandering down village streets where they meet with their mates.

> **Only the Portuguese could have created a dog such as the water dog – bred by Portuguese fishermen to have webbed feet.**

And when they do, the consequences are interesting. With dogs of all shapes and sizes everywhere, Portugal could win 'most bizarre dog-shape' competitions hands down.

Pampered dogs aside, the Portuguese have a fondness for animals as long as they are useful. Only the Portuguese could have created a dog such as the *cão d'água* – the water dog – a poodle-like animal bred by Portuguese fishermen to have webbed feet so it could help chase fish into the nets. Today the Portuguese

20

water dog is in demand mainly after President Obama bought one for his girls: as well as having webbed feet, the dogs don't moult so they make great pets for those who don't have time to vacuum.

The English expression 'You can't teach an old dog new tricks' has a Portuguese equivalent, *Burro velho não aprende* – an old donkey doesn't learn. While an Englishman will have or know someone with a dog, a Portuguese will have or know someone with a donkey. The faithful friend, guard and guide in England is an essential tool in Portugal: the donkey, mule and ox are the Portuguese tractor, plough, lorry and taxi.

Bulls are adored for their ability to fight. 'We're not like the cruel Spanish,' the Portuguese will claim. 'Our bullfighting is an art, our bull fighters don't kill the bull.' This, of course, is true: in the ring the bull is artfully goaded, speared until blood runs down its side, then hauled out of the ring – where it is discreetly butchered.

> **There is a saying that 'To be Portuguese means that the pet rabbit your child named on Thursday becomes dinner on Saturday.'**

However much a Portuguese may respect the usefulness of an animal, it is always tempered by the animal's unfortunate ability to taste good. There is a saying that 'To be Portuguese means that the pet rabbit your child named on Thursday becomes dinner on Saturday.' Most animals are considered fair game for the pot. Rabbit, hare, wild boar, pheasant, duck and partridge are all commonplace on restaurant menus, most of them blasted out of a nearby field. Any wildlife that isn't popular in the kitchen may be shot anyway, in case it eats things that are: the Iberian lynx and the much feared wolf are now both virtually extinct.

The Portuguese eat every part of the animal. Cow's hoof, sheep's head, chicken feet, testicles, gizzards and pig's ear salad are just some of the tasty morsels on many a menu, while meat stews can resemble the aftermath of an elaborate autopsy. Which is why another saying has it that 'To be Portuguese means every time you look at your dinner, there's something with eyeballs looking back at you.'

> **❝ Cow's hoof, sheep's head, chicken feet, testicles, gizzards and pig's ear salad are just some of the tasty morsels on many a menu. ❞**

Vegetarians are to be pitied. They cannot even trust a green vegetable soup known as *caldo verde* because of the large lump of ham that hides at the bottom.

The following recipe is for a dish called *papas de sarrabulho* (which feeds five). As well as a little flour, garlic and onion you will need: 0.5kg pork belly, 0.25 kg veal, 2 pigs' livers, 1 chicken thigh, 50g pig's tongue, 50g pig's heart, 200g pig's blood, 0.5 of a litre of red wine. Digest slowly and you will understand how the Portuguese truly appreciate animal life – preferably in the same dish.

Obsessions

The Three 'F's

The Portuguese have an expression *A tradição já não é o que era* – 'Tradition is not what it used to be' – and to get a handle on what it means to a Portuguese, you need to know what this phrase encompasses.

António de Oliveira Salazar, the dictator who ruled Portugal for much of the 20th century, encouraged his citizens to be patriotic: be loyal to Portugal and you don't have to worry what's going on elsewhere in the world. To do so he promoted traditional values, even striving to find the 'most traditionally Portuguese' village in the country. You would think he would have bestowed the award on some bright, white-washed fishing village overlooking the sea, but instead he awarded it to

> **❝ The carrot that was used to motivate them was the trio of Portuguese traditions – sport, music and religion. ❞**

Monsanto, an ancient mountain village close to the Spanish border where many of its hard-working residents live in houses that seem to grow out of the giant granite boulders that make up the local landscape.

Hard working and tough was an attitude he wanted to foster amongst his people, and the carrot that was used to motivate them was the trio of Portuguese traditions – sport, music and religion – promoted as the three Fs: football, *fado* and *Fátima*.

After Salazar's demise it took the nation quite some time to move on. Those elements the dictator had promoted as 'traditional' outsiders viewed as a land that time forgot, where the lifestyle seemed rooted in the early parts of a century that was nearly over. Even in the 1980s, Portugal had just one motorway – and that only partially linked Lisbon and Porto. In the countryside, horse-drawn vehicles were almost as prevalent as cars. Rural women still dressed in black for some seven years after the death of their husbands.

> **" Those elements the dictator had promoted as 'traditional' outsiders viewed as a land that time forgot. "**

Understandably there was a backlash against tradition and a craving for all things modern. Portugal is now a modern 21st-century EU state, with a maze of motorways and sprawling high-rise housing estates. The EU has taken away the *escudo* and brought in the essentials of the Euro economy: multi-national companies, chain stores, a world of gizmos and 24-hour television. Hence the lament: 'Tradition is not what it used to be.'

But all things are relative. Horse-drawn vehicles still rattle down rural lanes past elderly women dressed in black. Portuguese shops still often close for lunch and wrap your purchases in paper and string. Sundays are still quiet in towns and cities. *Fado*, viewed as old-fashioned for a while, is very much back in fashion, while football and religion never went out.

Football

You can often tell a lot about a country by the way its national team plays football. Brazilian football is showy, sexy, passionate and invigorating. Germans play with a ruthless functionality that is regularly successful. Russians play a collective team game that promises much but inevitably fails; the British play as if they're the best but never are. And the Portuguese? Their style can be summed up by the first year their most famous player, Cristiano Ronaldo, joined Manchester United. He would beat two or three players with dazzling skill, then fall flat on his face in front of the goal.

The Portuguese look good but are prone to breaking down at crucial moments, typified by their performance

> **66 Portguese footballers look good, but are prone to breaking down at crucial moments. 99**

during the European Championships of 2004. Hosted by Portugal in a series of glittering new stadiums the national team glided impressively into the final. But fate inevitably reared its head: they lost to underdogs Greece and the nation wallowed in a collective sea of *saudades*.

Portuguese males have an obsession with football.

Every restaurant, café and bar has a television in a corner showing football almost every night of the week. Not only are live matches shown, but also training sessions, practice matches and an endless series of pre- and post-match interviews. One of the country's best selling newspapers, *A Bola* (*The Ball*), is dedicated

> **66** Every restaurant, café and bar has a television in a corner showing football almost every night of the week. **99**

almost exclusively to football. Those who can't get to a match or a television will have a radio clamped to their ears on match days.

There is a restaurant in Faro called *Marisqueira Faro e Benfica*. This sums up the owner's priorities: he is proud of his seafood (*mariscos*), proud of his town (Faro), but equally proud of a football team, Benfica, even though it plays several hundred kilometres away in a different city.

Supporting a team in Portugal is a complex affair. If you are from Coimbra, you will follow the local team, Académica. Unless Benfica visit, in which case you will support Benfica. Or you may support the other, slightly less working class team from Lisbon, Sporting. Or perhaps the other big city team, Porto. While some countries' football supporters are fiercely tribal, if you are Portuguese you will support one of these big three teams: Benfica, Sporting or Porto. Bizarrely, even in Madeira, which is nearer to

Morocco than to Portugal, the islanders will switch allegiance from their local teams, Marítimo and Nacional, to one of the big three when they visit the island. It is for this reason that Portugal can boast the football club with the most supporters: Benfica's 160,398 official members puts it into the record books.

Unless two of the big three teams are playing each other – when fierce passions of rivalry are roused – Portuguese football matches are quite sedate, even civilised. Locals may

> 66 Even in Madeira, the islanders will switch allegiance from their local teams to one of the big three when they visit the island. 99

watch Braga play Olhanense, but no-one is too bothered who wins. Nevertheless, football matches are the best places to learn certain Portuguese phrases, largely involving questioning the referee's eyesight or the parentage of the opposition's strikers.

Fado

To be Portuguese you need to get something out of music that other nationalities don't understand. Unlike those peoples whose national music – bagpipes, say, or the French accordion – is part of a country's heritage, the Portuguese are hard-wired to *fado* at birth. It is a chord to their soul as rich, deep and satisfying as a cup of Portuguese coffee. Only perhaps in Greece would you hear the national music played pretty much wherever you go as you do in Portugal: on the radio, on buses, in taxis, cafés and restaurants, on TV or drifting from clubs in the streets, sometimes sung by buskers and street performers or even the odd talented postman.

Fado is a genre of Portuguese music that is taken extremely seriously. In 1974 when Portugal's army rebelled against the regime's orders to subjugate the independence movements of Portugal's colonies, the music of folk and *fado* singer José 'Zeca' Afonso acted as a trigger to what was subsequently called 'the Carnation Revolution', with rebels stuffing carnations down the barrels of tanks and guns that put up token resistance.

Fado means 'fate' and its themes are about how fate has foiled the singer in love and in life. There's a lot about '*a terra*' – the homeland that is missed because you or your lover are far away. No-one is sure of the origins of *fado*, but it seems to have been influenced by the songs of the slaves the Portuguese took away from their homes and families, and there are hints of Arabic and African in its melodies.

> **Fado means 'fate' and its themes are about how fate has foiled the singer in love and in life.**

Many performances are accompanied by the Portuguese guitar, a tortoise-shaped instrument with

12 steel strings. Portuguese emigrants to Hawaii in the 19th century took these guitars with them which ultimately evolved into the ukulele – and onwards to the altogether jauntier tunes of the likes of George Formby.

To be a *fado* singer, it helps if your name sounds a bit moody and miserable, hence the top *fadistas* are called

> **It is said that football is like religion, but for the Portuguese religion is like football.**

Mizia, Mariza and Mafalda. The greatest *fado* performer of all was Amália Rodrigues, who summed up the *fadistas* attitude when she said, 'I have so much sadness in me, I am a pessimist, a nihilist, everything *fado* demands in a singer I have in me'. Although born into poverty, Amália went on to become almost an ambassador for Portugal, performing *fado* all over the world and appearing in several films. She died aged 79 in 1999, an event which prompted three days of national mourning, before she was buried in Lisbon's National Pantheon, a lone queen alongside statesmen and heroes.

Fátima

It is said that football is like religion, but for the Portuguese religion is like football. If you like it, you have a passion for it and want to show it off at every opportunity. Visit many a home and the walls will be adorned with pictures of the Last Supper. Lorry drivers decorate their cabs with pin-ups of well-endowed women hanging next to images of the Virgin Mary.

Portugal does not have an official religion, though during the long years that Salazar was in power the assumption was that, just as every Portuguese man would have a moustache, all Portuguese were Catholic. In Braga, Portugal's most important religious centre, 90% of today's population claim to be Catholics though a truer picture may be drawn from the fact that the number of priests has dropped from over 1,000 in 1970 to around 500 today.

> **&6 Lorry drivers decorate their cabs with pin-ups next to images of the Virgin Mary. &9**

The church may not be quite what it was, but it is still a force. There's a saying in the Algarve that 'a weekend without sunshine is like a Sunday without a church service', and though this implies that you can rely on the weather, it also speaks volumes about the assumption that Sunday means church.

The true strength of the church is very evident during the pilgrimages to Portugal's most holy site at Fátima. Every May and October, hundreds of pilgrims descend on the small town, many having walked for miles to get there – the seriously devout completing the last few hundred metres on their knees. The faithful flock here because of the miracle that occurred in 1917, when an apparition of the Virgin Mary appeared before three local children. The town of Fátima has since blossomed into quite a resort, with hundreds of hotels, a museum filled with wax figures relating to the miracles, a Museum of the Apparitions which offers a mock version of Hell, and a myriad shops selling religious paraphernalia around the main square which is double the size of Saint Peter's Square in Rome. Portugal has created one of Europe's first religious theme parks.

Religion is big business in Fátima, but for most of the Portuguese religious sites and festivals offer as much the chance to relax as to commune with God. At another pilgrimage site in the north of Portugal, Bom Jesus, if you go behind the church you will find a big park with a lake: visit, pray and picnic on a day out with all the family.

> **For most Portuguese, religious sites and festivals offer as much the chance to relax as to commune with God.**

Religion's other main pull is tied up with every Portuguese's deep sense of superstition. At Amarante, the church of São Gonçalo contains the tomb of a saint famed for being able to sort out marriages: rub your hand over the tomb and you'll be lucky in love. So many people have done just that that the tomb has been worn smooth over the years. Give a Portuguese a reason to believe in something and you will rarely get half measures.

Records

As a country sitting at the periphery of a continent, it is easy for Portugal to get overlooked. So the Portuguese sometimes like to do things to get themselves noticed. This may be the reason they love setting a bizarre array of official records, especially when they can raise money for charity in the process. Amazingly they can boast the following, all of which were set in just two years from 2010 to 2011:

- the largest firework rocket (13.4 kilos, in Porto);
- the largest surfing wave (100 feet/30 metres high) in Nazaré, braved by a Hawaiian big wave rider);
- the largest gathering of bodyboarders (272 in Figueira da Foz 2011);
- the largest group ever to don red noses (15,959 people in Lisbon);
- the largest procession of people in Santa outfits (14,963 in Porto).
- the largest hair drying lesson (attended by 250 people, in Lisbon);
- the world's largest ever limpet rice dish, in a pan which weighed 850 kilos (Porto Moniz, Madeira).

Portugal also boasts the tree that produces the most cork (1.02 tonnes, produced by the Whistler Tree in the Alentejo district).

These records may not mean a lot to the rest of the

world, but they mean a lot to the Portuguese – just as a long flowing beard means a lot to a man with a bald head: it compensates for a lack of something more meaningful to boast about.

The Family

Children and marriage

An aspect of the Portuguese language helps one to understand Portuguese behaviour towards children. Essentially, all things small are good, kind, warm and pleasant. So when you say *obrigadinho* rather than *obrigado* ('thanks'), the diminutive *inho* (literally 'a little thanks') signifies an especially warm thanks. Ditto *ciaozinho* (a warm goodbye), *beijinho* (a warm kiss) and *inho* or *inha* (just-about-anything-else). In a restaurant, you can even ask for the *continha* (attractively small bill), though of course this may be wishful thinking.

66 By making things small you are comparing them to children, so by definition you are making them nice. 99

By making things small you are comparing them to children, so by definition you are making them nice. Children are simply adored in Portugal. When a woman gives birth, she is said to '*dar à luz*' (give to the light): children are magical, to be pampered and doted on at all times.

33

At midnight in just about any town in Portugal, children will be out and about, sitting with their families in restaurants or cafés or playing in the town squares. Unlike most English-speaking countries, children are not expected to go to bed early: they sleep when the parents sleep. There are no bars that are out of bounds to those under 18. Wherever you go, you will be faced with children and quite possibly children will be in your face. A Portuguese working family is just that: shops may be run by the husband and wife, with the older children helping out and the baby tucked in a cot behind the counter. Market stalls may be run by women with babes in arms. For a Portuguese to be childless is a condition to be pitied.

❝ Wherever you go, you will be faced with children and quite possibly children will be in your face. ❞

The pampering of children has two distinct outcomes. The first is that they are thoroughly spoilt. Toyshops flourish in Portugal as do amusement parks and playgrounds. Head to a shopping centre and it will have whole areas dedicated to children. The Colombo shopping centre in Lisbon even has roundabouts and a roller coaster.

The second outcome of pampering children is that they are expected to give something in return: a respect for their elders. Although you will find Portuguese children who are just as obnoxious and badly behaved as anywhere else, the majority are polite and respectful. The seeds have been sown for payback time for the adults which is nurtured by girls reading a series of books about a girl called Anita. Despite being about 10, Anita wears the sort of clothes that would certainly be provocative on an adult woman. She lives in an idealised Toy Town world of cuddly animals and spends most of her time tending to babies: the perfect mother in the making. In contrast, boys read *Ruca* by the Canadian Christine L'Heureux about a small boy who imagines a lot but does very little: the perfect father in the making.

> **It is said that you know you are Portuguese if the day after you get married, your spouse's entire family move into your house.**

As they grow up, children are expected to continue to love and respect their parents. They will probably stay with their parents until they find a spouse, and the potential spouse will need to be approved by the parents. When a boy is brought to a girl's home, the couple can go anywhere in the home – as long as one parent is between them.

It is said that you know you are Portuguese if the day after you get married your spouse's entire family move into your house: the in-laws are always in. For a man, the perfect wife will take on the role of his mother. The problem for the wife is that his mother will quite possibly be in the room next door.

The elderly

Some countries wheel away their elderly to over-heated homes where they see out their time in front of TVs or peering through gaps in net curtains. The Portuguese proudly wheel out their elderly to be admired in public.

Go to any village café or bar and you will see the elderly lined up at the outside tables watching the world go by or in animated conversation. Every shady bench in a village square will be kept warm by an elderly bottom or two. Stone tables in parks or at viewpoints will have a huddle of elderly men noisily playing cards. Indeed many rural villages seem to be run almost entirely by the elderly, the young having inconsiderately moved away to look for better things to do.

> **66 Every shady bench in a village square will be kept warm by an elderly bottom or two. 99**

Married couples often live with their parents and these parents eventually become elderly people: hence most elderly live with the family. The young of the family therefore see the grandparents as important figures in their lives. Their opinions matter, even if they are dated. This seems to help the elderly keep going: since the year 2000, there have been seven Portuguese who have lived to be over 110 years old (the oldest died in 2009 aged 115).

When you are Portuguese and old, you are said to

have reached a *terceira idade*: a third age. Like a political 'third way', it's a meaningless label, but it sounds a lot more glamorous and hopeful than 'old age pensioner'.

Manners

The Portuguese are like the country's weather: sunny and bright for 95% of the time, with the odd outburst of thunder and occasional patches of greyness. The latter manifests itself in the service industry where the rule seems to be: don't serve with a smile. This is particularly true in hotels and restaurants – the more expensive the establishment, the more expressionless the service must be.

Greetings and formality

Politeness and formality are very important to the Portuguese, but this does not mean they are never rude. If you point out that your beer is flat or your wine is corked, it is unlikely you will get an apology. In a conversation it is quite normal to interrupt a person who is mid-flow. But it is simply not done to use the wrong form of address when talking to a Portuguese. Like the French, the Portuguese use a *tu* form for friends and family and a more polite *você* form for those one does not know so well. The equivalent of Mr and Mrs is *Senhor* and *Senhora*, though if you know the woman well, you may call her *Dona*, for example *Dona* Ana. However, do not do the same for a man. If you call someone *Dom* Carlos, it means King Charles. *Dom* is strictly for monarchs.

Greetings are a similarly delicate labyrinth to negotiate. When adults visit their parents, they will greet them with a kiss on the cheek, or sometimes a hug and a kiss on each cheek if they haven't seen each other for some time. The same applies to good friends. With those less familiar it's a handshake. Or an appropriate 'hello'.

When greeting a child, you'll need to do a series of checks. For small babies, this involves gently pinching their cheeks while making gooey cooing noises. Ideally you'll also check the baby's weight by picking it up, swaying it about and then passing it around the room so everyone else can have a go. Toddlers are given similar treatment, though instead of merely picking them up, you'll probably hold them by the arms and swing them around before depositing them on the ground so you can check their sense of balance. Greetings for older children involve checking how well their hair sticks to their head: you'll need to rub their hair briskly with your hand until either the

> 66 You'll check the baby's weight by picking it up, swaying it about and then passing it around so everyone else can have a go. 99

children duck out of the way or their hair falls out.

Telephone greetings are altogether simpler. When you answer the phone you say '*Estou*' – which literally means 'I am' but is used to mean 'It's me.' This puts the ball firmly back into the hands of the caller, who has a tricky decision to make: whether to call you *tu*, *você*, *senhor*, *senhora*, *Dona* or, if you are royalty, *Dom*.

Systems

Under Salazar Portugal pretty much stood still for a large part of the 20th century. The advantage of this is that the nation has been able to take a bold step straight into the 21st century. In fact, the technological advances of the last few decades are remarkable. In the 1980s, a landline telephone was something of a rarity. Now most

> **66 ATMs not only dispense money but allow you to buy tickets for pop concerts and pay your gas bill. 99**

village squares are Wi-Fi hotspots, and even the humblest road sweeper will probably have a mobile phone. Lisbon and Porto have state-of-the-art metro systems, and ATMs not only dispense money but allow you to buy tickets for pop concerts, pay your gas bill, and generally ensure that your bank account is as empty as the country's coffers.

Portugal has reached bravely into the IT age, but it still has one foot firmly planted in the past. There are sleek new motorways that have tolls using the Via Verde system which reads a microchip on the dashboard to charge cars without them having to stop, but signs on motorways still warn people not to use them with a horse and cart. Restaurants have energy-saving lights that switch on when you enter the WC, but you still have to put your loo paper in a bucket because the drains can't handle it.

Transport

To travel on Portugal's roads is to know the raw mixture of danger and excitement experienced by the navigators of old, and the biggest test of your nerve is to be behind the wheel of a car. Like an explorer setting foot on foreign soil for the first time, you never know quite what to expect. In your rear view mirror there's quite possibly a fellow driver who is so close behind that you can read the numbers on his watch. Ahead of you, roads have a tendency to suddenly narrow or veer dramatically to one side. Other cars are likely to pull out in front of you even if it is clearly your right of way, and if it's not a car, it could be a lorry, a

> **To travel on Portugal's roads is to know the raw mixture of danger and excitement experienced by the navigators of old.**

tractor, a donkey and cart or a herd of cattle. Beware the exclamation mark sign beside the road. This perplexing warning always means something: you're just never sure what or how soon, but it will almost certainly mean that somewhere in the next few kilometres the road will be either dug up, sunk, pot-holed, closed by a landslide or possibly all four.

Obras (roadworks) are an ever present peril. Roads are rarely closed for them. Instead, you can drive for miles on the rough base of a dug-up road, dodging workmen, bulldozers and lorries tipping hot tarmac.

Because driving in Portugal is not for the faint-hearted, many people prefer to take public transport. This, too, is not always a straightforward experience. Trams don't so much drive around the hilly streets of Lisbon and Porto as sail round like ships on a wavy sea, the drivers turning wheels and levers like a captain struggling with a caravel in a storm. Buses, too, buck and sway through the city and the countryside alike, sending any loose bags and unwary passengers sliding across the floor like unsecured ballast. Perhaps because so many of their ancestors were navigators, Portuguese bus drivers still control their vehicles as if they expect the contents of the bus to be tied down, as on a ship.

> **"Trams don't so much drive around the hilly streets of Lisbon and Porto as sail round like ships on a wavy sea. "**

Road signs

Having been the greatest navigators on the planet, able to sail round the unchartered world and open up hitherto unknown sea routes, the Portuguese authorities assume that drivers don't need signs. Those that do exist tend to be so small that if you are going any faster than a donkey and cart (for which they were perhaps first designed), you won't be able to read them.

Recent road building has meant an increase in the number of signs, and some of these are even quite big. Unfortunately, when a new road is attached to an old one (as is often the case), the authorities become unsure of what to call it. So they may keep its old name, such as EN1455, but add a new name to it, such as A22. Some roads therefore have two or even three numbered designations. And even these are inclined to peter out after a promising start, leaving the driver with a bewildering choice at unsigned junctions or alarmingly diverging motorway lanes.

66 Occasionally signs are as good as you could wish for, as long as you are heading in one direction. 99

Occasionally signs are as good as you could wish for, as long as you are heading in one direction. If coming from the opposite direction, there is no sign at all. And this isn't to do with traffic priority, but seemingly because either the sign-makers forgot to print both sides, or because the organisers assumed that the traffic would mostly be coming from one direction.

All this means that arriving at your destination in Portugal feels like a Vasco da Gama moment: the triumphal end of an epic voyage.

Rules

The Portuguese are fond of rules. It is said that Bartolomeu Português, a 17th-century pirate famed for wreaking havoc amongst Spain's ships in the Caribbean, established the Pirate's Code – a set of rules widely adopted by any self-respecting terror of the seas.

Visit a beach in Portugal and you will be faced with a sea of signs telling you not only what you can do and where you can swim, but also when you can swim: take a dip outside the 'official swimming season' from June to September and you will be considered mad, or a foreigner.

66 In an old-fashioned bar you will see not only 'No smoking' but 'No spitting'. 99

In an old-fashioned bar you will see a plethora of signs – not only 'No smoking' but *'Não cuspir'* (No spitting). You can rarely enter a public convenience without being faced with signs warning you not to throw anything down the lavatory that doesn't come directly from your body. And there are various unwritten

43

rules that are expected to be observed, such as that for women over a certain age who are expected to wear fur until at least the end of May when it is deemed to be warm enough to cast it aside, and for girls under a certain age – usually marriageable ones – who are expected to stay at home in the evening even if their younger brothers are allowed to go out.

But rules are only rules up to a point. The 'official' times posted in the windows of restaurants, cafés and tourist offices are rarely adhered to: people open up when things seem busy or the sun is out, and shut down when things are quiet or it's raining. Breaking traffic regulations on the road is par for the course. When a former Prime Minister was spotted lighting a cigarette on a plane to Venezuela, it was shortly after his government had implemented a ban on smoking in public places. A Portuguese does not so much disobey rules as reinterpret them.

> 66 The 'official' times of cafés and offices are rarely adhered to. 99

Rubbish

There are rules designed to restrict the *porcaria* (filth) that industries and individuals like to leave around the place, but few are adhered to. Perhaps to reduce the amount of rubbish their bin men have to collect, and hence minimise the noise they make, a significant number of the Portuguese do not place their litter in bins but find places to leave it that are altogether quieter. Areas by the sides of roads are always handy; the edges of out-of-town car parks can be useful, while attractive woodland is ideal. Picnic spots are also good dumping grounds. The Portuguese love a good picnic, especially if it is at a beauty spot where you can park your car within two metres of a picnic table. Picnics tend to be prodigious affairs, with enough food and drink to feed all the family which can equate to the size of a small army. Once over, there's a varied array of rubbish to dispose of, so to be considerate to the next picnicking family, this is discreetly put behind a bush or perhaps a tree trunk – wherever the previous visitors left theirs.

> **66 The Portuguese associate green with the colour of their flag rather than with the environment. 99**

Ecology

The Portuguese associate green with the colour of their flag rather than with the environment. This is despite the fact that the Portuguese government has invested heavily in renewable energy. Wind turbines march over once barren mountain ranges, solar panels glint from the roofs of many new buildings and one of the world's first wave farms was pioneered off the coast in the north.

People are encouraged to remember the three Rs: *reduzir, reutilizar, reciclar* (reduce, reuse and recycle),

> **66 For most Portuguese, recycling means reusing your plastic water bottles to fill up for free from a local spring. 99**

but for most Portuguese, recycling means reusing your plastic water bottles to fill up for free from a local spring, or your empty wine bottles to decant from the cheap plastic flagons you buy from the supermarket. In Portugal these matters are more economical than ecological. Never mind saving the planet – saving euros is the only reason to be green.

Leisure & Pleasure

Festivals

The best time to witness Portuguese togetherness is at one of the countless *festas* or festivals that punctuate the calendar. The Portuguese celebrate just about anything: from opera, rock or jazz to the cinema, the sea, gay pride or flowers; from famous saints (Anthony, John, Paul) to extremely obscure saints (have you heard of Saint Ovídio, the patron saint of ears?). Whatever the label, the *festas* all follow pretty much the same format: a chance for a 'knees-up' where all the locals can come together and share food and liberal amounts of liquid. People of all ages, from toddlers to middle-aged couples to tottering grannies, jig happily to boppy folk music in a wobbly mass of togetherness.

Only the Portuguese could devise a festival that requires youths in replica football shirts to be armed with over-sized plastic hammers, and yet not end up with a riot. The youths are encouraged to hit over the head with the hammer anyone who is attractive or female, preferably both. Though this would result in mass arrests in many northern European countries, it passes off without a murmur each year for the festival for São João in Porto.

> 66 People of all ages, from toddlers to middle-aged couples to tottering grannies, jig happily to boppy folk music in a wobbly mass of togetherness. 99

Food is another major cause for celebration. As you would expect, there is a festival for sardines and festivals for wine, but there are also others for virtually any foodstuff you care to mention. The Algarve region alone has specific festivals for the smoked sausage, the *cataplana* (a stew cooked in a wok-like dish), the octopus, beer, smoked ham, seafood, *petiscos* (tapas-like snacks), sweet potatoes, chestnuts, and barnacles. These festivals give thanks for various harvests and for times when certain foods are at their prime, and like other Portuguese festivals, are a blend of the religious and the secular.

Perhaps the most bizarre festival is during the Festas de São Bartolomeu in the village of the same name in the Minho district. Families with sick children traditionally come here each August for the annual Banho Santo. This involves the sick child circling the church three times with a cockerel tied to his or her head, before being dipped three times in the sea – a kill-or-cure approach followed by the usual medley of song and dance.

Holidays

In 2011, a plan to 'get Portugal back to work' meant a series of tough austerity measures – and the one that was hardest to swallow was the decision to axe three public holidays. But the Portuguese still take around ten national days a year, not to mention the odd regional holiday.

> **The Portuguese try to spend as much time away from work as at it.**

The Portuguese claim to have a healthy balance between work life and leisure time. This is because they try to spend as much time away from work as at it. The generous number of public holidays certainly helps. And when the public holiday falls on a Thursday, for example, it is normal to take a 'bridge' day: there's not much point in going to work on the Friday. Ditto Tuesday: you may as well take off Monday. And if the public holiday falls on a

Wednesday, why bother with Monday and Tuesday. Or perhaps Thursday and Friday. Hell, why not take the whole week off?

Fishing

Remarkably for a country where fishing is a major source of employment, the Portuguese also love fishing as a hobby. The best fishing spots are usually on the most remote, inaccessible stretches of wave-battered coastline. To reach them means either casting your line from a cliff where one false move would mean instant death, or clambering down from on high to some slippery rock where you cling on for dear life until some fish takes your bait. This may sound risky but because every time you get in a car to go anywhere in Portugal you risk being mown down, when you take up fishing any worries about risks seem insignificant.

> **66 The working day is unsullied by namby-pamby naps. Instead they keep going through the power of caffeine. 99**

Café culture

Unlike their soft Spanish neighbours, the Portuguese don't really bother with siestas. Admittedly, lengthy lunch breaks can roll on well into the afternoon, but the working day is unsullied by namby-pamby naps. Instead, they keep going through the power of caffeine.

Coffee culture is serious business in Portugal. This is not surprising as it was the Portuguese who ensured that there has always been a lot of coffee in Brazil: allegedly, a Portuguese colonist took the first coffee plant to Brazil from French Guiana in 1727, and within a century coffee had become Brazil's biggest export.

Coffee 'menus' long predate the fad for skinny lattes and flat whites that have permeated other cultures. A Portuguese coffee drinker has the choice of a *bica* (espresso), *garoto* (small white coffee) *galão* (a big milky coffee), *chinesa* (a big black coffee), *carioca* (a weak black coffee) and quite a few more. Most pure-blooded Portuguese punctuate their working days with coffee breaks every hour or two, starting at breakfast and ending last thing at night. Any outsider doing this with a *bica* will probably be buzzing for days, but the Portuguese thrive on it, doubly so when the coffee is accompanied by a liberal dose of sugar.

> **66 Most pure-blooded Portuguese punctuate their working days with coffee breaks every hour or two, ending last thing at night. 99**

It is said that every Portuguese's secret ambition is to run his own café, and it would seem that a good proportion of the population has realised the dream. In any major city a café can be found every few hundred yards, and in small villages cafés comfortably outnumber things like hairdressers or bookshops. And all provide the real thing. The humblest kiosk, the most pokey café, the smallest museum will have a gleaming chrome espresso machine using freshly ground coffee beans. While the French are said to introduce their children to alcohol by giving them watered-down wine, the Portuguese do the same with milky or watery coffee. You can't become a true grown-up Portuguese without a caffeine habit.

Sex

On one level, the Portuguese are very open about sex. Naked women are ten a penny when it comes to advertising shampoos or shower gels. Scenes of a sexual nature are shown on TV with barely a bat of an eyelid at a time of day well before what is considered decent in the UK, and at the cinema, graphic sex is quite OK for films shown to 16-year-olds. But what goes on the screen stays on the screen. In real life, an element of prudishness remains from the

> **Topless sunbathing on most Portuguese beaches is on a par with mooning: it just isn't done.**

repressive regime when kissing in public was frowned on. Topless sunbathing on most Portuguese beaches is on a par with mooning: it just isn't done. 'Girly' magazines are rarely visible in any newsagents, top shelf or otherwise, and though sleazy dives certainly exist, they are mostly well hidden: even the larger cities don't have blatant red light districts. If they do become too blatant, something is done about it. In Bragança, there was an influx of *meninas brasileiras*,

> **66 Portuenses see Lisboetas as lazy do-nothings and call them *alfacinhas*, lettuce eaters. 99**

Brazilian prostitutes who plied their trade a bit too brazenly in the cobbled streets of this northern town. Local women made a stand against them, accusing the *meninas* of corrupting their menfolk. Within a few years, the majority of the prostitutes had been hounded out by the local women, while the local men were left – literally and metaphorically – with their tails between their legs.

Humour

The butt of most Portuguese's jokes are people from the country's different regions. There is a saying that Porto works while Lisbon plays: Lisboetas see their Portuense rivals as dull Jacks who only work, and call them *tripeiros*, tripe eaters. Portuenses see residents of the Portuguese capital as lazy do-nothings and call them *alfacinhas*, lettuce eaters. Inhabitants of the Alentejo region in the deep rural south of the country are regarded as slow country bumpkins, hence: 'Why do the Alentejanos plant garlic at the side of the road?' 'Because it's good for the circulation.'

People from Madeira are laughed at for their funny accents. Those from the Azores are even slower country bumpkins with even sillier accents. People from the Algarve are thought of as mean and are said to 'eat out of a chest-of-drawers', so if an unexpected guest arrives the drawer can be shut and the food is out of sight.

A Portuguese can be fiercely proud and patriotic, but can also follow the saying, 'Never take yourself too seriously, and mock those who do.' Thus the biggest butt of a Portuguese's jokes is the Portuguese themselves. For example:

- Tavares was driving to the northern beaches when he saw, beside the road, a sign:

  'Warning: dangerous turn to the north.'

  So he, being a safe person, went south.

- A Portuguese book-keeper asked his boss: 'Our files are full: should we throw away the old reports?' 'Yes,' said the boss, 'but first make a copy of them.'

- A Portuguese sees a Coke vending machine for the first time. It's wonderful: feed in a token, and out rolls a Coke. Two tokens, two Cokes. Ten tokens, ten Cokes. So he goes up to the store owner and asks for another 50 tokens. The man says, 'At this rate, I'll soon be clean out of tokens.' 'Maybe,' replies the Portuguese, 'but while I'm on this winning streak, I won't stop.'

Culture

Museums

The Portuguese simply love museums: you will find one in virtually every town of any size and though none of them is quite as wild as Iceland's penis museum or Copenhagen's museum of pornography, there is an amazing range of themes, from tiles to olive presses, from pharmacy to freemasonry, cork to immigration, bread to match-boxes. Many don't really have a theme at all: regional museums just bung in whatever seems remotely old or interesting.

> **66 Regional museums just bung in whatever seems remotely old or interesting. 99**

Lagos's museum has everything from Visigothic coffins to deformed animal fœtuses, straw hats and stuffed goats. Vila Flôr in the Trás-os-Montes region displays antelope-horn furniture and an embalmed Angolan rat.

Decorative art

If a building is worth having in Portugal, you stick tiles on it. A glazed expression is what you adopt when admiring *azulejos*, the glazed tiles that were first introduced by the Moors but have since become an essential part of the nation's art: the tiles are decorated with elaborate patterns, motifs, battle scenes, and just about anything else. While most European churches show off their stained glass, Portuguese churches show off their tiled panels which decorate not only the inside but often the outside of church buildings. Other countries use tiles for bathrooms and perhaps the inside of a butcher's shop, while the Portuguese stick tiles on town halls, fountains, car parks, mansions, underpasses, motorway bridges and blocks of flats.

The tiles help insulate buildings from the weather, fires, and perhaps most importantly, graffiti. The Portuguese seem to have a Banksy living on every corner. There is an astonishing

> **❝ The Portuguese stick tiles on town halls, fountains, car parks, mansions, underpasses, motorway bridges and blocks of flats. ❞**

variety of elaborate graffiti on virtually any non-tiled building surface in Portugal, from simple colour squiggles to photographically realistic images, and from grotesque parodies of people to imaginative graphics. The train line from Sintra to Lisbon has a virtually unbroken sequence of graffiti along its entire length, which takes almost 50 minutes to admire.

Literature

If there's one art form the Portuguese are proud of it is literature. You cannot be Portuguese unless you have read *The Lusiads*, Luís de Camões' epic poem narrating Vasco da Gama's sea voyage to India, complete with tales of sea monsters. Portugal's Jane Austen is Eça de Queirós, whose studied portraits of life in 19th-century Lisbon are every bit as witty. Then came Fernando Pessoa, clearly an eccentric and ahead of his time in creating avatars (he wrote under a series of alter egos, the first one at the age of six), but whose musings on the meaning of life mean

66 Portugal's greatest writers are glorified wherever you go in the country. 99

that he is remembered as a Modernist genius. José Saramago continued with the torch of experimentalism, writing whole books without any punctuation and one, *Blindness*, without naming a single character. The current golden boy is José Luís Peixoto who writes fractured mosaics of books that are like assembling a jigsaw.

Portugal's greatest writers are glorified wherever you go in the country. Statues commemorate their places of birth and death. The football team from the town of Barcelos is even named after a writer, Gil Vicente.

When Saramago won the Nobel Prize for Literature in 1998, Portugal was deeply honoured that one of its writers had been acknowledged by the outside world. The Portuguese usually celebrate their own art and culture so fulsomely in the knowledge that no-one else will.

Style and taste

The Portuguese have a sense of style that is roughly in inverse proportion to their income. The poorest Portuguese have taste and style by the bucket-load. Visit a country worker and you'll find a home brimming with clever and tasteful ideas: tiny windows artfully trimmed with dazzling blues or yellows, humble patios warmly swathed in dazzling geraniums, modest porches bedecked with hanging baskets and wind chimes, whitewashed internal walls studded with understated paintings or minimalist religious icons.

The middle classes have a more questionable taste, with a fondness for dark wooden furniture whose polished surfaces are protected by a lacy army of crocheted doilies, probably made by grandma.

Go to the home of a wealthy Portuguese and generally all sense of taste and style has been thoroughly flushed away. Giant edifices are surrounded by anodyne gardens neatly trimmed of any interest, with gravel drives and over-pruned bushes. The houses are all windows and walls in greys, browns and creams, their uplights and elaborate gateways a sterile show of wealth. Inside you'll find outlandish furniture, bland modern art and oversized ornaments. The inhabitants have arrived at a state far removed from their cultural background: a euro-fuelled euro-home.

> **❝ The Portuguese have a sense of style that is roughly in inverse proportion to their income. ❞**

Customs

Superstition

The Portuguese are superstitious. In Porto and Lisbon, people consult gypsies who read their palms or sell them sprigs of lucky heather. Rural areas are steeped in tales of spirits and *lobisomens* (werewolves) and many houses – notably in the southern Alentejo district – are rimmed with blue paint which is said to keep off the evil eye. It's still not unknown for country people to pick up the phone to the local village healer (*curandeira*) rather than the local GP.

The Catholic church doesn't exactly encourage these beliefs, but recognises that superstition and religion are so intertwined that you may as well be resigned to it. There are many *curandeiras* who

> 66 The Catholic church recognises that superstition and religion are so intertwined that you may as well be resigned to it. 99

believe they are given healing powers by God and use a mixture of prayer and alternative medicines such as herbs and potions to do their deeds. If you tell them you have a sore stomach, you'll be treated to a gentle massage of the abdomen before leaves are placed over the sore spot: if the leaves have dried out in a day or two (a distinct possibility), the cure has worked.

If you are Portuguese and pregnant, don't carry furry animals during pregnancy or your child will be born hairy. Nor is it a good idea to wear flowers in your hair or your child will have a birthmark. But if the child is born with a fœtal membrane over its face, rejoice: this is a sign it will have special powers to be the next *curandeira*.

Many church altars are piled with the limbs and heads of plastic dolls, or prosthetic arms – the donor believing that the church can cure the

> **If you are Portuguese and pregnant, don't carry furry animals during pregnancy or your child will be born hairy.**

part that has been left there. On the island of Porto Santo, it is the sands of the golden beach that offer miracle cures for skin complaints, hence the surreal sight of elderly people buried up to their necks in the sand.

Then there is Sebastianism. Dom Sebastião was a young king who saw himself as a daring crusader and set off to do battle in Morocco in 1578. His army was trounced and Sebastião was never seen again. Without a legitimate heir to the throne, within two years Portugal had fallen under Spanish occupation, but the Portuguese believed (or hoped) that Sebastião would return and take back the throne some misty day. When Portugal regained its independence from Spain in 1640, the new king João IV promised to relinquish the throne should Sebastião reappear, even though he would have been pushing 90.

Although the Portuguese have given up on Sebastião

actually rising again – and have done away with the monarchy altogether – Sebastianism remains a belief that a mythical king will return one day to lead Portugal to greatness once more.

Sebastianism can also be a term of mockery. If you say Portugal's football team will win the World Cup, or that Portugal's economy will soon be booming, you will be accused of being a Sebastianist: a wishful thinker with his head in the clouds.

Names

Notable Portuguese have had their names passed on to streets, a dish of clams and a crater on the moon. In Lisbon, there's a road called Rua Comandante Ruben Auber Tavares de Melo. This fact tells you two things: 1) that you often need a large envelope to accommodate people's addresses and 2) that the road took its name from an important historical figure, a fact you can deduce from his name.

> **Parents often ask their young children to reel out their full names as if it were a party trick.**

Portuguese names tend to be very long. Parents often ask their young children to reel out their full names as if it were a party trick (and for the best ones, it often is). When Manuel Gomes marries Maria Silva, the family name becomes Silva Gomes. The process continues, so that a Silva Gomes marrying a Ferreira becomes Silva

Gomes Ferreira and so on, though there is an official limit of four surnames. But the aristocracy, no doubt wanting to prove how important their family lines are through history, often sidestep this legislation and proudly maintain surnames that support five, six or more. For example, the 19th-century Duke of Saldanha's registered name was João Carlos Gregório Domingos Vicente Francisco de Saldanha Oliveira e Daun. The longer the name, the more likely it is that that person has an illustrious pedigree.

> **The Registry Office has a list of approved first names, each with an agreed official spelling.**

This seemingly logical system has a fluidity that in fact can totally obfuscate a family history. Take a name such as Maria Ana Pimenta Costa Rocha. Without knowing the family, it would be impossible to know if Maria took Rocha from the father and Pimenta Costa from the mother, or the other way round. Or she could have taken Costa Rocha from the father and Pimenta from the mother, or the other way round. Another possibility is that Pimenta, Costa or Rocha were part of a grandparent's surname, which either parent would be entitled to use even if it were not part of their current surname. Clear? Probably not.

First names are somewhat simpler. The Registry Office has a list of approved first names, each with an agreed official spelling. Not surprisingly, Catholic names predominate. You will find several villages in Portugal called Seismarias which take their name from the *seis* (six) Marias who at one stage lived there, quite possibly all from the same family. Maria, Ana, Paula, João (John), José (Joseph) and Paulo are all safe Portuguese mainstays.

Straying from the list can be problematic and requires an official declaration before it will be allowed. A foreign resident of Portugal visited the town hall to register the birth of his daughter. Luckily he knew what to expect and was fully prepared:

Father: I'd like to register the birth of my daughter, who was born yesterday.

Registrar: You need the certificate from the hospital proving she was born.

Father: Here it is.

Registrar: You need the mother's ID card.

Father: Here it is.

Registrar: And a photocopy.

Father: Here it is.

Registrar: And who is the father?

Father: I am!

Registrar: I need your passport.

Father: Here it is.

Registrar: And a photocopy:

Father: Here it is.

Registrar: What name do you want to register as?

Father: Anya.

Registrar: Let's change that to Ana.

Father: No, Anya.

Registrar: We only have Ana.

Father: But we want her to be called Anya!

Then followed a pantomime '*No, you can't,*' '*Oh yes I can*' about registering the name Anya. Eventually, upon examining a declaration from the British Consulate, the registrar relented and the official registration process could finally commence.

> **Perhaps because first names are relatively restricted, many Portuguese adopt or are given nicknames.**

Perhaps because first names are relatively restricted, many Portuguese adopt – or are given – *alcunhas* (nicknames). So someone of German descent may be known as *alemão* (the German), the local bread maker may be known as *padeiro* (the baker), a hairless man may be known affectionately as *careca* (the bald) and so on. Footballers are particularly keen to be known by nicknames. It's a habit long prevalent in Brazil, e.g. Pelé – real name Edison Arantes do Nascimento. World renowned Portuguese football player Cristiano Ronaldo dos Santos Aveiro is known to all as Ronaldo, the name allegedly given to him by his father who admired US actor Ronald Reagan. Former Porto star (real name Givanildo Vieira de Souza) admired for his stocky strength, is known simply as Hulk – though he has enough modesty not to add Incredible.

Health & Hygiene

Cleanliness

Although they have an inclination to dispose of rubbish in public places, the Portuguese like to keep things clean. In fact the proverb 'cleanliness is next to godliness' was probably invented by the Portuguese. The mornings in most towns and cities begin with every shop and café getting a thorough sweeping and mopping out, including the area of pavement in front. In the big cities at night you will hear the hum of street cleaners giving the roads a good seeing-to. Most houses are tiled throughout and thus easy to clean with a regular sweep and a sloosh with a wet mop.

In parts of southern Portugal, citizens are encouraged to keep the outsides of their houses spotlessly white, too. The town of Serpa, in the Alentejo, even ran a competition for the 'whitest street of the year' with plaques to commemorate the winners. Public conveniences, too, are kept sparklingly clean. Most have a permanent staff of women who sit by the entrance awaiting tips, between ensuring that any germs visitors may introduce are annihilated with an array of bleaches and fluids. The biggest danger in visiting a public toilet in Portugal is not from germs, but from inhaling toxic fumes.

> **66 The proverb 'cleanliness is next to godliness' was probably invented by the Portuguese. 99**

Sickness

When it comes to health, 'gripe' is common in both the English and Portuguese sense (where it means 'flu'): everyone likes nothing better than to complain about it – even though the Portuguese lifestyle may be largely to blame.

Another concern is high blood pressure. The biggest causes of death in Portugal are strokes and coronary disease and most people are aware of the link with arterial tension. Many pharmacies have machines that can test your blood pressure and they are so popular that queues often form to use them. Sales of test-your-own-blood-pressure kits have gone through the roof.

Look inside a Portuguese person's medicine cabinet and you will most likely find pills and potions for coughs and colds because the Portuguese

> **66 Machines that can test your blood pressure are so popular that queues often form to use them. 99**

are paranoid about *correntes de ar* (draughts), which they are convinced could bring about your early demise. In winter, when cold Atlantic winds blow, this is perhaps no surprise, considering that the heating in many houses consists of little more than a lukewarm electric radiator. But in summer, the obsession continues. Even with the thermometer pushing 30°C, many people will prefer to keep their windows firmly closed 'in case there's a draught'.

Babies are believed to be particularly vulnerable to cold air. When taken out for a walk in a buggy, it is essential that the infant be swaddled in as many layers as possible. Babies and children must also wear hats at all times. In winter, hats keep the draughts off a child's head, and in summer they keep off the sun. Take a hatless child down a street in Portugal and sooner or later someone will berate you for it.

66 Take a hatless child down a street in Portugal and sooner or later someone will berate you for it. 99

Around any museum you'll see long lines of school parties, each child wearing their school's mandatory hat. Schools don't allow children in the playground without one.

The only time this rule is waived for children is when they are on a bike. Despite the distinct possibility that the child's head will become acquainted with a lamppost or passing car, hats and helmets are seen as unnecessary when cycling. Luckily, Portuguese medicine cabinets are also well stocked with iodine to treat any resulting cuts and wounds.

Exercise

The Portuguese have a strict Saturday exercise regime. The morning warm-up involves slow stretches in the kitchen as you prepare an elaborate picnic. For your dose of fresh air, you drive somewhere with the picnic in the boot, parking the car as near as possible to (or preferably at) a beauty spot. Then you feel the burn with your main workout, which involves unloading the picnic from the boot and putting the food out on tables. After all that tiring activity, you have earned the right to spend the afternoon with your family devouring what you have brought, after which you will be too tired to put anything but the essentials back into the boot: the picnic debris can stay where it is, admiring the view.

The other main source of exercise is going to the beach. Again, it is important to park the car as close as possible to the patch of sand you intend to occupy. A hefty workout is had putting up the sun umbrella, ambling down to the sea and immersing yourself in a few Atlantic breakers, after which you will need several hours to recover. A good way to do this is to lie prone under your sun umbrella or, ideally, to visit the local beach restaurant for a filling meal to replace any calories you may have lost.

> **66 A hefty workout is had putting up the sun umbrella... 99**

Of course there are ultra-fit Portuguese who take part in 'real' sporting activities at weekends, and a growing number use the cycle paths that are springing up around the country. However, the reduction in coronary disease that cyclists enjoy is more often than not counterbalanced by the increase in cyclists' deaths bought about by alcohol-fuelled drivers.

Teeth

Dentists get fed up to the back teeth in Portugal as their patients' tooth care is so bad. A recent study of children in one area of Porto reported that 70% had cavities and nearly 40% needed urgent treatment. This is partly a hangover of people's perception that a visit to the dentist portends an emptying of the wallet: most Portuguese dentists are private, and free check-ups for children are a relatively recent innovation. For adults, some public sector workers have dental treatment paid as part of their healthcare, but the majority have to pay for it. So, many don't.

As most Portuguese are *gulosos* (sweet toothed) and simply love sweet pastries, cakes and sugary desserts, the tooth fairy is kept extremely busy, and not just for children.

If you have a sweet tooth in Portugal, it can be good news, as this implies you have at least one tooth left.

Eating & Drinking

Portugal had fast food long before the international chains made their appearance on European shores. *Pregos* and *bifanas* are beef or pork steaks in a bun and are far tastier than American burgers. Every town has its restaurant serving sumptuous grilled chickens, which outdo anything served in Kentucky.

Portuguese navigators are credited with introducing foods that are now associated with other countries' cuisines. Chillies were taken from the Americas to the East by the Portuguese, and the word 'vindaloo' derives from *vinho* (a wine) and *alho* (garlic) sauce from Portuguese Goa. Japanese tempura derives from the deep fried method of cooking things introduced by the Portuguese. Despite their influence on world cuisine, world cuisine has made little impact on the Portuguese table. Brazilian dishes like *feijoada* (bean stews), *rodizio* (barbecued meats) and *picanha* (strips of garlicky beef) are popular, but that's about as exotic as Portuguese restaurants get.

> **❝ Despite their influence on world cuisine, world cuisine has made little impact on the Portuguese table. ❞**

The author Robert Wilson pertinently wrote 'The quickest way to get trampled to death is to come between the Portuguese and their lunch.' The Portuguese take their meals seriously. Breakfast is unnecessary as it takes up some of the space required for long and leisurely midday meals. Most lunch breaks last around two hours, and there is invariably a lot of eating to be done. If you eat in a restaurant, grilled fish and meat dishes are routinely accompanied by rice or chips or quite often both. However, some unwritten law states that certain fish should only be served with boiled potatoes – ask for chips to come with your *pescada cozida* (boiled hake) and you'll be considered peculiar. There is also a rule which states that very few dishes should be tainted with vegetables. If you must consume vegetables, it's best to have them mashed to a pulp in a soup, which many Portuguese have as a starter to line their stomachs for the meal to come.

While you are waiting for your main course, the waiter will assume you need something to keep your hunger at bay. You will therefore be presented with a basket of bread, a bowl of olives, and a selection of starters which may be a whole cheese, a plate of prawns, sausage, sardine pâté or an elaborate medley of seafood. By the time you have had your starter and bowl of soup, your appetite should be whetted for the main event, which could well be a colossal plateful consisting of two or three pork steaks served with rice and chips and salad. And that's before the dessert menu makes an appearance.

> **If you must consume vegetables, it's best to have them mashed to a pulp in a soup.**

A Portuguese dish, *pescada cozida com todos* consists of boiled hake with boiled potatoes and vegetables: healthy eating personified. But this is a rarity. Every Portuguese restaurant may serve more or less the same thing, but the Portuguese know what they like: cholesterol-ridden, calorific comfort foods par excellence.

Favourite foods

If your Portuguese spouse tells you 'I really want to sink my teeth into some nun's belly', do not be overly alarmed. Whether it was because of a need for money, or out of boredom or divine inspiration, Portuguese nuns excelled in producing cakes and desserts – and you can still get them today, many retaining their risqué names. So you can eat *Barriga de Freira* (Nun's Belly), *Colchão de Noiva* (Bride's Mattress), *Pudim do Abade de Priscos* (Priest's Pudding) or *Papos de Anjo* (Angel's Crops). Most of these are made with a mixture of egg and sugar: sticky concoctions that are a dentist's nightmare but which are a firm favourite with the Portuguese.

❝If you are Portuguese, you don't waste anything that can be eaten. ❞

Another favourite is a sauce called *açorda*. For this a farmer will combine stale bread with whatever can be foraged from the land – birds' eggs, wild garlic, wild herbs – and mix it up to create a tasty mushy sauce commonly served with prawns. If you're Portuguese, you don't waste anything that can be eaten.

Most essentially, you will have a developed taste for *bacalhau*: dried salted cod. This is the national dish, though the uninitiated may well be alarmed by its uncooked form as it resembles a slab of grey cardboard and smells like old socks. Despite its mummified appearance, that piece of *bacalhau* being offered for sale does *not* date back to the 1500s when it first became popular amongst sailors who found that, by salting and drying the fish, it could be preserved for long and arduous journeys overseas. The Corte Real brothers have a special place in Portuguese hearts as it was they who perfected the curing art, having sailed as far as Newfoundland for its rich cod banks.

Once salted and dried, this *fiel amigo* (faithful friend) goes through an elaborate process to make it palatable. You have to soak the stiff slabs of fish in water for up to two days before removing the skin and bones from the swelled and softened flesh, which is then boiled and strained into a fishy pulp. From this, the Portuguese are able to conjure a reputed 365 different *bacalhau* dishes, one for every day of the year, including *rissóis de bacalhau* (cod rissoles), *bacalhau com natas* (baked with cream) and *bacalhau à brás* (with fried potatoes, olives and egg).

> ❝ The Portuguese are able to conjure a reputed 365 different *bacalhau* dishes, one for every day of the year. ❞

The most important meal for the Portuguese is eaten on Christmas Eve. On this special day they will prepare a special, favourite treat. What is it? A recipe involving *bacalhau*.

Drinks

In a country as hot as Portugal, water is important so the Portuguese know their mineral waters. You do not ask for any old water but always name what you want: Serra da Estrela (from the mountains), Pedras Salgadas, Pisões, Vidago, Vitalis and many others, each known for their mineral content.

Even with water, water, everywhere, you can always get a drop to drink. A Portuguese's annual consumption of alcohol outdoes the good folk of France and Spain, but binge drinking is not an issue. Alcohol is treated as a necessary fluid to help with the digestion of your large meals. Weekday lunches are filling meals washed down with at least one carafe of wine,

> **66 Alcohol is treated as a necessary fluid to help with the digestion of your large meals. 99**

and probably followed by a coffee and brandy. Weekends are synonymous with long leisurely lunches liberally lubricated with wines and liqueurs. Many workers kick off proceedings much earlier in the day, visiting a café for a coffee and glass of something even more warming before work.

Any bar you enter will be lined with an impressive selection of firewaters and liqueurs made from some unlikely ingredients: *brandymel* (brandy with honey), *ginginha* (a cherry liqueur served with the whole cherry, stone included), *amêndoa amarga* (made from almonds), *medronho* (the fruits of the strawberry tree). What a Portuguese cannot eat he will distil. Even the grape skins discarded from the wine presses are fermented and made into a highly alcoholic firewater called *aguardente*.

The most popular drink to have with a meal is wine. Wine critics are, of course, good at identifying specific grape varieties. 'Definitely a pinot noir,' they'll say, or 'A fine cabernet sauvignon.' In Portugal, however, the critic will have to say 'Definitely *Bastardo*' or 'I detect a touch of Dog Strangler.' Most regions of Portugal have their own grape variety, often unique to that area – and with names like *Bastardo*, *Tinto Cão* (Stained Dog), *Rabo d'Ovelha* (Ewe's Bum) and *Esgana Cão* (Dog Strangler), it is no wonder that wine growers have resisted the urge to introduce dull old chardonnays or merlots. And Portuguese wine tends to be so full, fruity and drinkable that it is hard to resist the urge to call, 'Waiter? Another Ewe's Bum, please.'

What is Sold Where

Shopping

The Portuguese love shopping which is why there are so many mega shopping malls – some of the largest in Europe – to cater for this passion. As well as shops, these malls have cafés, restaurants, cinemas and children's play areas, which means that all the family can happily spend the day there – which they frequently do.

In spite of the prominence of giant malls, Portugal's love of shopping ensures that independent shops thrive. Most town centres retain a comforting medley of traditional shops including a butcher, a baker, perhaps a candlestick maker, which somehow manage to survive even though they close for two hours at lunchtime, all day Sundays, probably Saturday afternoon and quite possibly another afternoon in the week. These shops maintain the art of customer service to the point that, whatever you buy, they will giftwrap it, even if it's a postcard which you promptly have to unwrap to write.

66 Shops maintain the art of customer service to the point that, whatever you buy, they will giftwrap it. 99

The Portuguese love a bargain. You can pick up inexpensive clothes, toys and knickknacks at weekly markets. Cheapest of all are the shops run by Chinese where everything is around one euro, from plastic washing up bowls to cheap imported toys that barely last a week before breaking.

But if the Portuguese want something enough, they don't care about the cost. And the objects of their desire are usually electronic goods. Whatever a Portuguese's income, it is essential that he or she has the latest model of microwave, DVD, flat screen TV, fridge and coffee maker. Despite these items being more expensive than many folk can afford, the wonders of the credit card make all this possible. The movie actor Errol Flynn could have been describing the Portuguese when he said, 'My problem is reconciling my gross habits with my net income.'

Fruit and vegetables

Give the Portuguese a patch of land and they will grow something. It may just be a stalky cluster of greens or a splurge of scarlet geraniums, but they have a knack for conjuring something from even the dustiest, most barren-looking soil. Portugal is a hard, arid land in the main, yet somehow generations of Portuguese have eked a living from it.

> **66 They have a knack for conjuring something from even the most barren-looking soil. 99**

In the north, it is traditional for the sons to inherit a share of their father's land – which has meant ever-decreasing patches of real estate. Go to a weekly market in the north of Portugal and you'll see the produce from these titchy holdings: a bunch of carrots here, a handful of cabbage leaves there, just about enough to subsist on.

In the south, various schemes have been tried for larger scale projects, for example, wheat, eucalyptus plantations and barley, but without much success. The Portuguese know their land: it is fertile if treated right, which means long waits and low yields from the likes of vines, olive trees and cork. Every town and village has its weekly market where local farmers sell their produce: all fresh, mostly organic, and the sort of satisfyingly irregular shapes and sizes that supermarkets dare not sell.

Fish and seafood

The country's fish markets have an astonishing array of fish harvested from the Atlantic and the country's rivers. And with so much of it, it is not surprising that the Portuguese are good at preserving any excess. There are shops that specialise entirely in tinned fish, from sardines and mackerel to squid, salmon and just about any other sea-beast you can think of. If you can put something in a can, the Portuguese can – and do.

Government & Bureaucracy

Politics

Portuguese politics have been exciting, especially since the birth of the republic in 1910. During its first 16 years of existence, it had no fewer than 45 changes of government. Perhaps tired of voting in so many elections, Salazar decided to be the one and only permitted Prime Minister. He lasted from 1932 until 1968, his party only relinquishing control after the Carnation Revolution. More political turmoil ensued when the lurch to the political left after the years of a right-wing dictatorship alarmed the establishment Archbishop of Braga enough for him to call the struggle as being like 'Christ against Satan'. When moderate socialist Francisco de Sá Carneiro became Prime Minister in 1980, his death in a plane crash a few months later inspired several conspiracy theories, and counter-revolutionary trials rumbled on until the 1990s.

> **❝ Since the 1990s Portuguese politics have become reassuringly dull... a few years of left-of-centre followed by a few years of right-of-centre. ❞**

Since then, Portuguese politics have become reassuringly dull. Its governments have settled into the pattern familiar in many EU countries: a few years of left-of-centre followed by a few years of right-of-centre, each government headed up by a middle-aged man about whom no-one seems to care much.

In 2011, Portugal elected Pedro Manuel Mamede Passos Coelho as Prime Minister (with a name that length, clearly someone from a good family). However, it would seem that the Portuguese no longer take politics very seriously, as the simplified English version of first and last name would identify him as Pedro Coelho. It is hard to take seriously a Prime Minister whose name translates as 'Peter Rabbit'.

Bureaucracy

The Portuguese like to follow the Keynesian idea that you can power an economy by hiring people to dig holes and then fill them up again, often, it seems, quite literally. It is pointless hiring one person to do a job quickly when five people can do it just as well over a much longer duration.

The Portuguese have perfected the art of bureaucracy. If you need to do some building work, for example, you may need a permit from the town hall to put up scaffolding, particularly if it blocks a public pavement. This is how to obtain it:

> **❝It is pointless hiring one person to do a job quickly when five people can do it just as well over a much longer duration.❞**

Go into one town hall department to get a paper to hand to a second department that can give permission to have a copy of where you plan to put this scaffolding. Take this copy of the plan and a paper to give to department one, to show you have received the plan. Get an invoice from department one to take to the accounts department. Pay the accounts department and receive three receipts. Take one to department two, who will give you a piece of paper saying they have received the receipt to give to department one. Give the receipt and the piece of paper to department one and then, finally, receive the permit to put up the scaffolding. Permit cost: 96 cents. Time taken: 3 hours 45 minutes.

Because it can take so long to get a permit to get things done, it is often easier to either offer a *lembrança* (backhander), or do the work without a permit in the knowledge that the bureaucracy involved to get a fine paid will take so long that it may well be forgotten.

Business

Getting work

Portugal produces around 50% of the entire supply of the earth's cork which is impressive, until you remember that the cork oak can only be stripped of its bark once every nine years. That's a lot of waiting for your cash crop. Portugal's other main crops – citrus fruits, olives and grapes for wine – are at least annual, but this is still a lot of waiting time for the average farmer. No wonder most of Portugal's workforce prefer the more regular income provided by the service industry, heavy industries or local businesses.

> **It helps to be part of a large family if you want to get on. Nepotism and cronyism aren't so much crimes as necessities.**

Most businesses in Portugal are family-run. So it goes without saying that it helps to be part of a large family if you want to get on. Nepotism and cronyism aren't so much crimes as necessities.

Portuguese business bows to the saying, '*A grande nau, grande tormenta*', literally 'To big ships, big storms'. Small and medium-sized enterprises are the norm: why bother with risky growth when an SME boss earns more than enough for a big car and a beachside villa?

However small Portuguese companies are, it does not stop them from thinking big, and for a Portuguese, thinking

66 However small Portuguese companies are, it does not stop them from thinking big. 99

something is grounds enough to advertise it as a reality. When a Portuguese company says it is developing a site somewhere or opening a new branch, it is announced as a fait accompli. The reality is that it is probably an idea on the drawing board, almost certainly without planning permission and quite possibly without funding.

Meetings

Meetings are arranged with polite formality. But the person who is holding the meeting must keep everyone else waiting. To turn up on time is a sign of weakness as it suggests the person isn't very busy and has time on his hands. When you meet a business person, shaking hands is customary, even if you've met the person several times before. But a presidential hand on the shoulder shows who's the boss, and you may well be guided into the meeting room like a ship into harbour.

The Portuguese business person is charm personified, but beware of the Portuguese desire to please. Business people have a tendency to say what they think you want to hear and will be reluctant to give you any concrete information. For this reason, business meetings are rarely conclusive. For a company to put all its cards on the table is considered an unnecessary risk in case they reveal a flaw in the company. Instead the Portuguese prefer to go on a charm offensive, and if they decide they like you as a person you are more likely to get what you want.

> **66 Business people have a tendency to say what they think you want to hear. 99**

But even then, don't assume that what is agreed in a meeting will come to pass. What seemed a done deal may later prove to be a starting point. Nothing is certain until a contract is signed. As a result, you'll probably come out of a meeting less clear about things than when you went in.

Titles

When football manager José Mourinho first left Portugal to become manager of Chelsea Football Club, the British press was aghast when he called himself 'the Special One'. In Britain this was seen as arrogance, but in Portugal there is nothing wrong with blowing your own trumpet. If you have something to boast about, shout it from the rooftops. And because status is important, use any titles you have.

However obvious they may seem, job titles are held in high esteem. On the television news in Portugal, reporters are always credited with their name and the word '*Jornalista*' afterwards. While English-speaking countries acknowledge a doctor's name and title, in Portugal you should similarly address journalists, teachers, lawyers, engineers, writers and poets – as well as professors and doctors. Members of Parliament – and even a few company bosses – are expected to be addressed as *Vossa Excelência* (Your Excellency).

Doctors are not necessarily medical doctors. Everyone with a first degree may be called *senhor douto*r (doctor). They have had the sort of education that has set them apart from Portugal's sea of illiterates, and they want you to know it. The Portuguese have an expression for it: '*Quem sabe, sobe,*' he who knows goes up.

> **66 Job titles are held in high esteem. Members of Parliament are expected to be addressed as *Vossa Excelência* (Your Excellency). 99**

Plain *Senhores* and *Senhoras* are expected to show deference to those with titles. Although Portugal booted out its dictatorial government, dictators still dominate in the boardrooms. Workers are not expected to challenge the authority or decisions made by the bosses. Should something go awry, the decision maker will quickly find a scapegoat – a lesser manager or the competitor, or the government. Taking personal responsibility for a problem is not an option.

Luckily, their skill at *desenrascanço* often comes to the fore in tricky situations. When something goes wrong, the Portuguese are bound to find a way to overcome it, even if the solution is a makeshift one that defies all business models.

Multi-tasking

Multi-tasking is an alien concept in Portugal. When walking, a Portuguese will even stop to talk to the

> **66 Multi-tasking is an alien concept in Portugal. When walking, a Portuguese will even stop to talk. 99**

person they are walking with: walking and talking is akin to multi-tasking, which is far too hard to co-ordinate. To multi-task means you are probably not doing your job properly: if a job is worth doing well it should be done properly, and in Portugal that means one thing at a time.

The only professional people who seem able to multi-task are taxi drivers. Portuguese taxi drivers can multi-task with astonishing efficiency. They have perfected the art of adjusting their seat belts, setting the taxi meter, talking to (while looking at) a client – even if they are in the back seat – all at the same time. They can even speed up while they do it. This multi-tasking mayhem must surely mean they are a race apart.

Language

If you know a Latin language, you will probably find much that is familiar in written Portuguese. Take the verb to love – *Amo, Amas, Ama, Amamos.* It may seem remarkably similar to what you learnt at school. But as is often the way in Portugal, all is not quite what it seems. Listening to Portuguese is an altogether different experience from seeing it written down: little is phonetic so what is on the page often bears little resemblance to what you hear.

66 The language is notoriously difficult to learn – not just for foreigners, but for the Portuguese themselves. 99

An estimated 220 million people speak Portuguese, making it the third most-spoken European language (after English and Spanish) and around the sixth most-spoken language in the world. This is despite the fact that the language is notoriously difficult to learn – not just for foreigners, but for the Portuguese themselves. Mistakes in spelling – and in particular the use of accents – are common: do you say *porque* or *por que*, is it *bóla* or *bola*, *selos* or *selós*? This may explain why 80% of Portuguese adults have a low level of literacy (compared with 25% in Sweden for example). However, when you speak Portuguese, it is important not to use one word when ten will do nicely: just like the people, who like to take their time over things, a sentence will wend its way slowly towards its conclusion.

The bulk of Portuguese speakers are in former colonies, the majority being Brazilians who inject their own joie de vivre into the language. Brazilian Portuguese has taken a different direction in other ways. As with American English, there are different words for the same thing and a tendency to simplify spellings. But while the British would never dream of adopting the American way of

66 When you speak Portuguese, it is important not to use one word when ten will do nicely. 99

simplifying the language of Shakespeare, the Portuguese are more pragmatic: as of 2011, traditionally awkward Portuguese spellings were given the boot in favour of the simplified Brazilian variants: so *óptimo* (very good) and *baptismo* (baptism) became *ótimo* and *batismo*. The modern Portuguese alphabet has also been lubricated with the addition of K, Y and W which previously did not exist as official letters. True to their nature, the Portuguese accepted these changes with relative calm.

Unlike the French, the Portuguese are not too concerned by the ever-growing dominance of English. Though English words are used for many computer terms, the Portuguese are pretty adept at coming up with their own ones for technological advances. For example, they call the Space Shuttle *Vai e vem* (go and come back) and a mobile phone is a *telelele*.

> **They call the Space Shuttle *Vai e vem* (go and come back) and a mobile phone is a *telelele*.**

The Portuguese may have been inventive navigators, but they were not inventive linguists. 'I think we'll call this island Wood' was as imaginative as the founders got for Madeira – which means 'wood'. Similarly when they found the Azores (named after the goshawks that they saw there), they named the mountainous island Peak (Pico) and the flowery one Flowers (Flores). 'What about the third one?' someone must have asked. 'A good idea' was perhaps the reply, 'We'll call it Terceira' (the third).

And so across the globe there are Brazilian cities called Big River (Rio Grande) and River of January (Rio de Janeiro), a Canadian region called Worker (Labrador) and a South African region called Christmas (Natal). About as poetic as the Portuguese got was the Cabo de Boa Esperança (Cape of Good Hope).

The Author

Born in London and now resident in Dorset, Matthew Hancock is a freelance journalist and editor. He graduated in English literature before teaching English in Athens, London and Lisbon. He felt he really got to know the Portuguese after walking the entire 775-mile length of the Portuguese-Spanish border, a three-month experience that made him realise you are rarely more than 10 miles from a decent café anywhere in the country. He has since visited virtually every Portuguese town of any note while researching the *Rough Guides to Portugal, Lisbon, Madeira* and *The Algarve*.

As a devotee of Portuguese literature he prefers reading Saramago to Dickens. But when he doesn't mind if Portugal's national team beats England at football, he worries that his fondness for all things Portuguese may have gone too far.

Xenophobe's®
guides

Available as printed books and e-books:

The Albanians	The Japanese
The Americans	The Kiwis
The Aussies	The Norwegians
The Austrians	The Poles
The Belgians	The Portuguese
The Canadians	The Russians
The Chinese	The Scots
The Czechs	The Spanish
The Danes	The Swedes
The Dutch	The Swiss
The English	The Welsh
The Estonians	
The Finns	
The French	**Xenophobe's®**
The Germans	**lingo learners**
The Greeks	
The Icelanders	French
The Irish	German
The Israelis	Greek
The Italians	Italian
	Spanish

Xenophobe's Guides

The Italians

Italians grow up knowing that they have to be economical with the truth. All other Italians are, so if they didn't play the game they would be at a serious disadvantage. They have to fabricate to keep one step ahead.

The Aussies

The Aussies do not wave like any other nationality. The movement they call their 'salute' is a constant hand wave in front of the face. Quite by chance this keeps the flies off their faces.

The French

French politicians look smart because power itself is chic, attractive, seductive, and one should dress to look the part. The French electorate would never allow any government to intervene in their lives if it were shabbily dressed.

The Canadians

Taming a savage wasteland can give anyone a feeling of omnipotence. Thus fearlessness characterizes many Canadians' behaviour. They will say 'I can do anything', with a sense of imperviousness and impunity.

The English

The English share a dislike of anyone behaving in a manner that 'goes too far'. The admired way to behave in almost all situations is to display a languid indifference.

The Americans

The American language embraces the bias towards good feelings. Stocks that plummet to half their value aren't losers, they're 'non-performers'. Someone doesn't have a near brush with death; he or she has a 'life-affirming experience'.

Xenophobe's® Guides e-books are available from Amazon, iBookstore, and other online sources, and via:

www.xenophobes.com

Xenophobe's® Guides print versions can be purchased through online retailers (Amazon, etc.) or via our web site:

www.xenophobes.com

Xenophobe's® Guides are pleased to offer a quantity discount on book orders. Why not embellish an occasion – a wedding goody bag, a conference or other corporate event with our guides. Or treat yourself to a full set of the paperback edition. Ask us for details:

Xenophobe's® Guides

telephone: +44 (0)20 7733 8585
e-mail: info@xenophobes.com

Xenophobe's® Guides enhance your understanding of the people of different nations. Don't miss out – order your next Xenophobe's® Guide soon.

Xenophobe's Guides